Lightwaves

Bob Chilcott

for SATB (with divisions) and piano

vocal score

MUSIC DEPARTMENT

OXFORD
UNIVERSITY PRESS

OXFORD

UNIVERSITY PRESS

Great Clarendon Street, Oxford OX2 6DP,
United Kingdom

Oxford University Press is a department of the University of Oxford.
It furthers the University's objective of excellence in research, scholarship,
and education by publishing worldwide. Oxford is a registered trade mark of
Oxford University Press in the UK and in certain other countries

First published 2021

Impression: 1

ISBN 978-0-19-353530-5

Music and text origination by Katie Johnston
Printed in Great Britain on acid-free paper by
Halstan & Co. Ltd, Amersham, Bucks.

Contents

Composer's note

Lightwaves was written for the youth choir festival in Eugene, Oregon, **picfest**, a festival with which I have had a long and happy association. Way back in 2016, the Festival Director, Peter Robb, and I discussed the idea of me writing a piece with the poet Charles Bennett on the theme of light. We saw the idea as a way of projecting light, in both a physical and metaphorical sense, as a positive force in our world. The texts touch on stars, the guiding light of a lighthouse, the electric light bulb, and the sun. The final song speaks of the light needed for trees to grow, a particularly emotive and pressing theme as I write this in autumn 2021.

The five songs have various voicings within the SATB format, so there is flexibility to perform them separately or as a set.

Lightwaves was composed as part of the new **picfest Commissions Project** for *Lift Every Voice 2020*, a festival in Eugene, Oregon. The event features youth choirs from across North America and around the world. Funding for **picfest's** innovative commissioning model pairs a Principal Patron with the Festival Chorus, whose members serve as both individual Singer Patrons and the ensemble premiering the work.

The choirs comprising the 2020 Festival Chorus were: Cantabella Children's Chorus (California); Children's Chorus of Maryland; Columbia Choirs (Washington); Emerald Valley Honor Choir (Oregon); Phoenix Boys Choir (Arizona); Pacific Youth Choir (Oregon); and The St. Louis Children's Choirs (Missouri).

Three months before the curtain was slated to rise on the festival, COVID-19 exploded onto the world stage, resulting in an historic shutdown of public gatherings and shuttering of performance venues. The premiere of *Lightwaves* was postponed until a return to choral events was possible.

At the time of publication, plans are underway for **picfest** to resume festival presentation with *Lift Every Voice 2022*. The premiere will add a second group of choirs as additional Singer Patrons. The names of both 2020 and 2022 Festival Chorus members and their choirs can be found at picfest.org/singer-patron/

Duration: *c.*15 minutes

Composed as part of the picfest Commissions Project for 'Lift Every Voice 2020'

Lightwaves

Charles Bennett (b. 1954)

BOB CHILCOTT

1. Telescope

Printed in Great Britain

OXFORD UNIVERSITY PRESS, MUSIC DEPARTMENT, GREAT CLARENDON STREET, OXFORD OX2 6DP

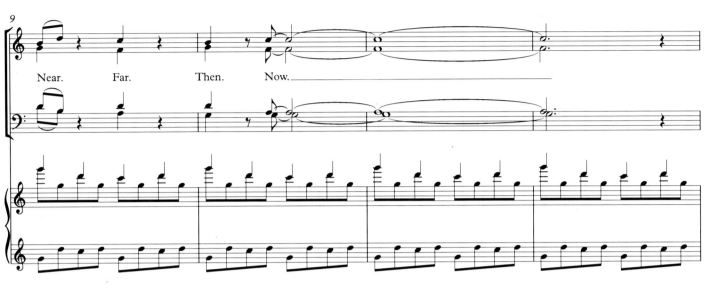

Near. Far. Then. Now.

Soon. Late. Dim. Bright.

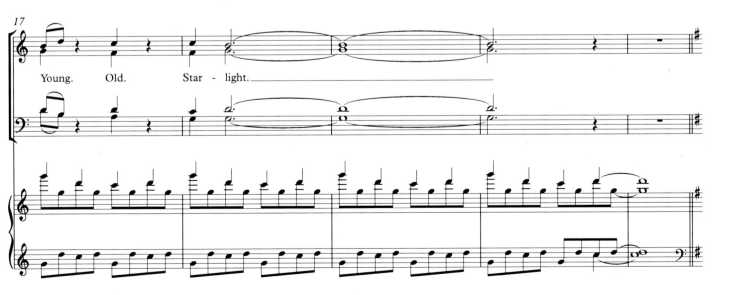

Young. Old. Star - light.

22 Here is light from a dis - tant star come to be where you are.

26 How far it trav - elled, what it passed, does not mat - ter, it's ar - rived at it's ar - rived at

30 last, ar - rived at last. Light from a star dis - tilled by time en - ters your eye,

ex - cites your mind. Light from a star dis - tilled by

en - ters your eye,

time en - ters your eye, your eye, ex - cites your

mind.

mf

UPPER VOICES (SEMI-CHORUS)

Dis-tant. Close. Fast. Slow.

Dis-tant. Close. Fast. Slow.

Near. Far. Then. Now.

Near. Far. Then. Now.

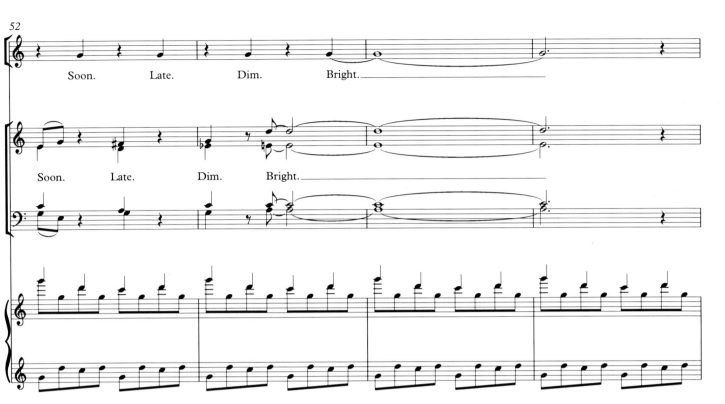

Soon. Late. Dim. Bright.

Soon. Late. Dim. Bright.

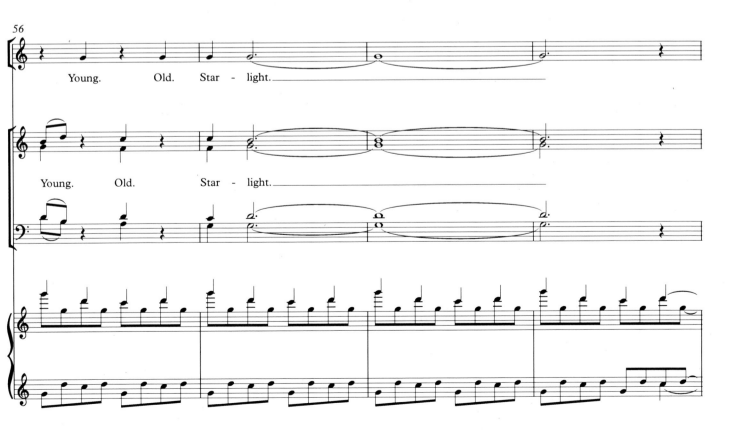

Young. Old. Star - light.

Young. Old. Star - light.

Im - ag-ine stars_ as_ thoughts that flash In the night as they pass.

from_ a star._____

Bright for a mo - ment, here_ you are, filled with won - der from_ a star, from_ a

star. Light from a star_ dis - tilled by_ time en-ters your eye,_ ex - cites your_

Dis-tant. Dis-tant.

Dis-tant. Dis-tant.

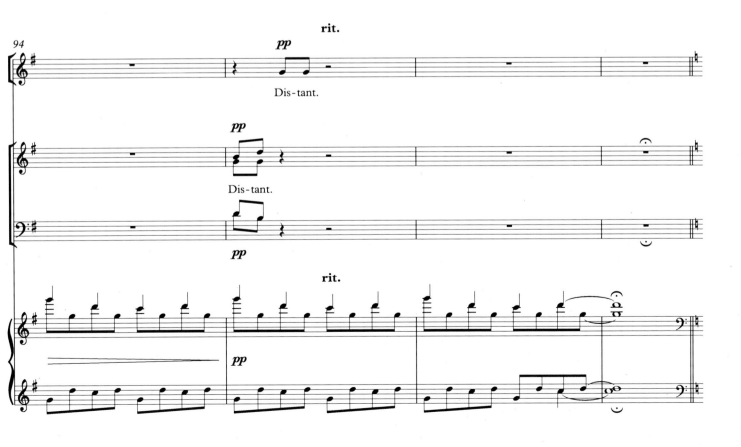

Dis-tant.

Dis-tant.

2. Harbour

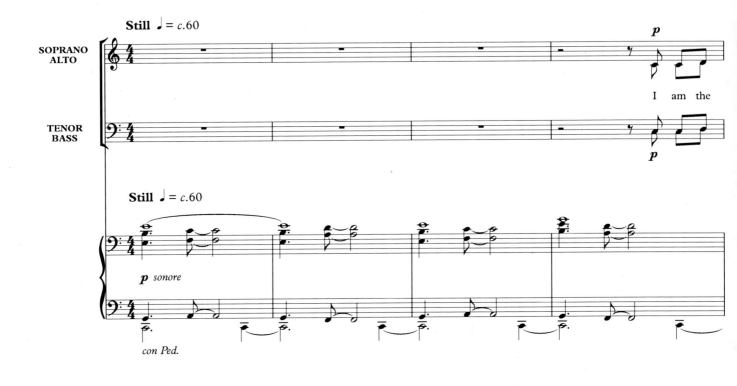

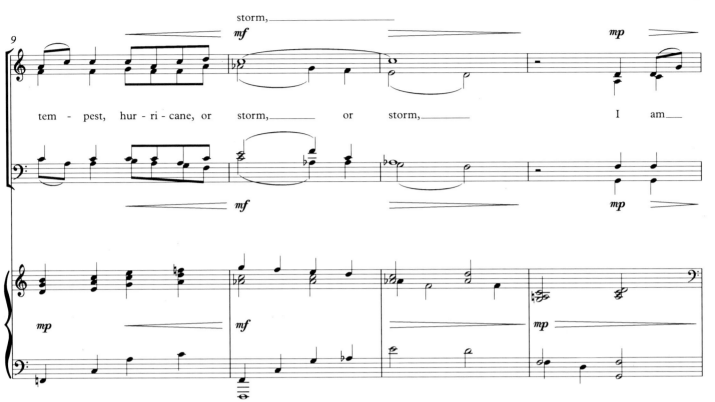

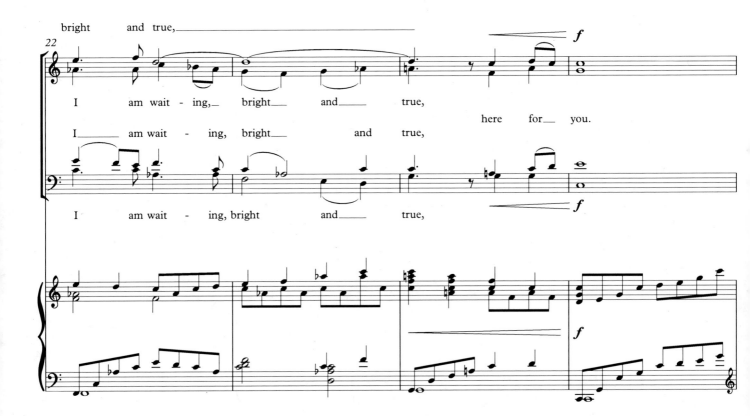

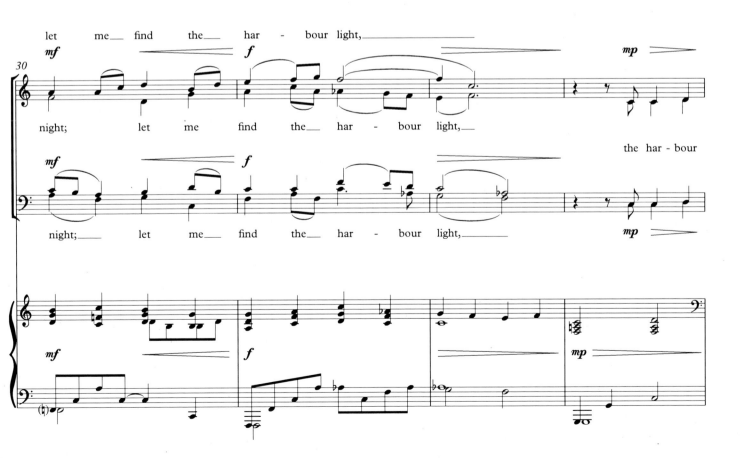

light._____ Time to leave__ those waves__ be - hind,__

UPPER VOICES (SEMI-CHORUS)

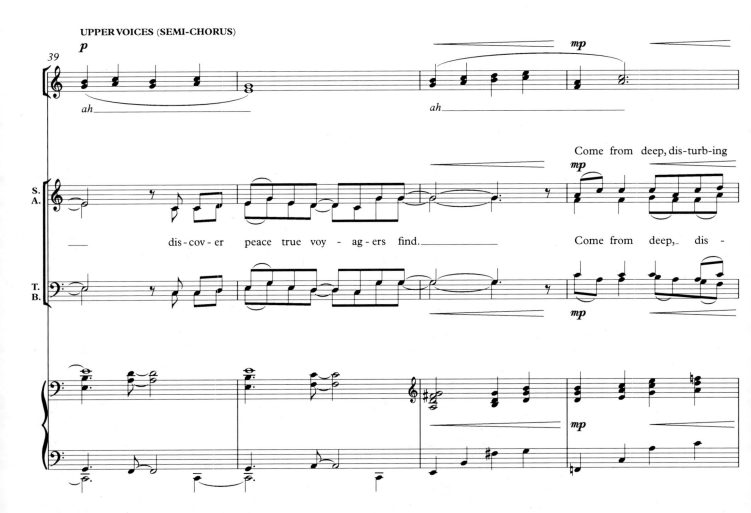

ah_____ ah_____

Come from deep, dis-turb-ing

dis - cov - er peace true voy - ag - ers find._____ Come from deep,__ dis -

3. Bulb

With energy ♩ = c.108

SOPRANO
ALTO

E - lec - tri - ci - ty, how I wish I

un - der - stood your shock - ing kiss._____ Po - si - tive, ne - ga - tive,

black or red, cut the wire, be - side my bed._____

con Ped.

room. In the dark_____ of morn - ing you

are my win - ter dawn._____

E - lec - tri-ci-ty, how I wish I un - der - stood your shock - ing kiss._____

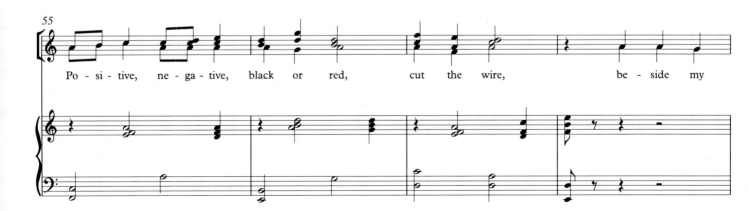

Po - si - tive, ne - ga - tive, black or red, cut the wire, be - side my

bed. You fell si - lent

once when the lines went down.

You are the i - dea I have when all my thoughts are

o - ver. Com - f'ta - ble to - geth - er,

like a hap - py cou - ple. At the end of the

day_____ you watch me sleep._____

E - lec - tri - ci - ty, how I wish I

un - der - stood your shock - ing kiss._____ Po - si - tive, ne - ga - tive,

4. Sundown

Hy-dro-gen storm! Play - time's o - ver: time to come down, come down. Feel the wa - ter,

smooth as silk, like Cle - o - pat - ra, sink in milk. I will heal your

wounds and bless skin that craves a sweet ca - ress.

Sky - swim-mer! High - ris - er! Eye - in - the - sky!

Sweet - sur - pris - er! Bob - by be - daz - zler! Hy - dro - gen storm!

Play - time's o - ver: time to come down, come

down. Be - drag - gle gold - en fea - thers now

61 in my bri-ny un-der-tow.___ Come on in, the wa-ter's cool,___

65 plunge in - to my swim-ming___ pool. Sky - swim-mer!

69 High - ris - er! Eye - in - the - sky!___ Sweet - sur - pris - er!

72 Bob-by be-daz - zler! Hy-dro-gen storm! Play - time's o - ver, o - ver.___

5. Leaf

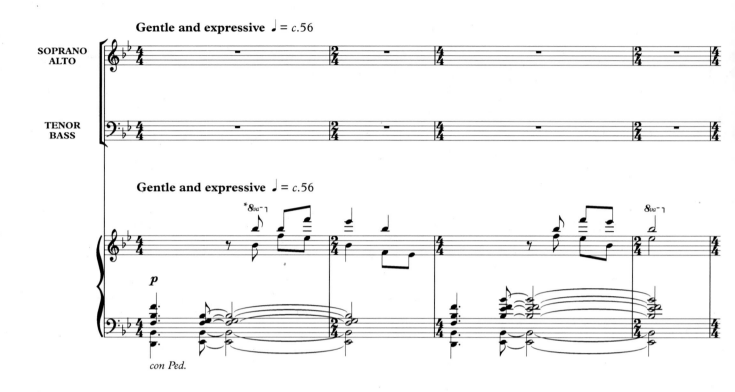

*The *8va* instruction only applies to the uppermost note of the chord.

O - pen in spring. Drop like a tear.

My days are short. They come and go. I feed on light,

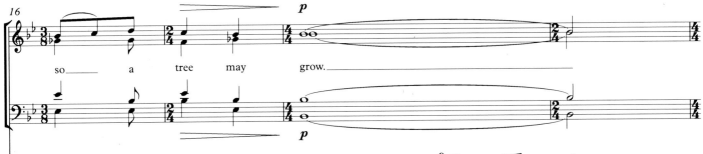

so a tree may grow.

TENORS & BASSES *unis.* *p*

Some-times I wish our skin could

un - der-stand the light the way a tree does, the way a tree__ does.

S./A. *unis.* *p*

The light would be our food, all na - tions on Earth would be a for - est,_____ be a

for - est. Per - haps we'd be___ wis - er at last,_____ dis -

Per - haps we'd be___ wis - er, wis - er at___

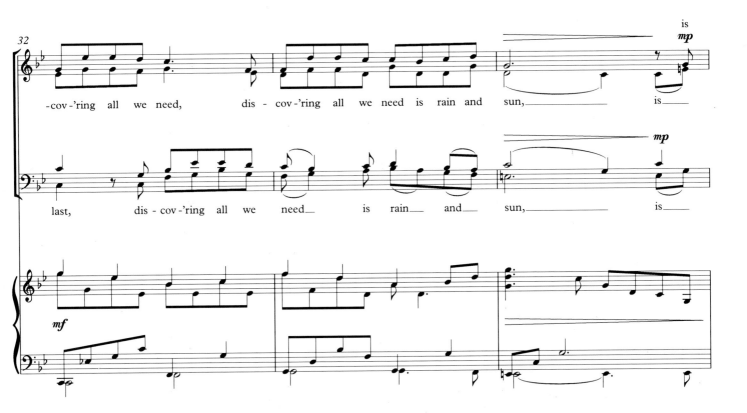

-cov-'ring all we need, dis - cov-'ring all we need is rain and sun,___ is

last, dis - cov-'ring all we need___ is rain___ and___ sun,___ is___

rain_____ and__ sun.

rain_____ and__ sun.

We'd

mp

breathe the Earth____ clean____ as we turned__ il - lu - mi -

mf

mf

mf

-na - tion in - to en - light - en - ment, en - light - en - ment,

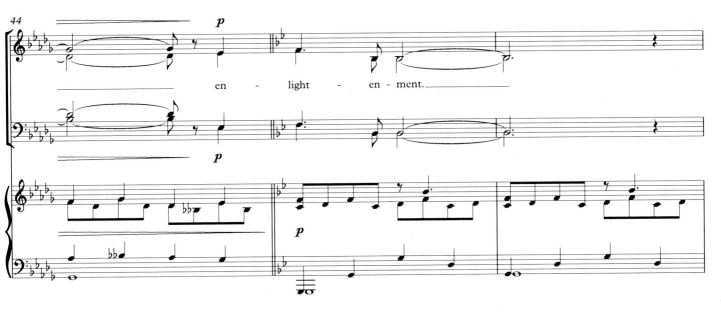

en - light - en - ment.

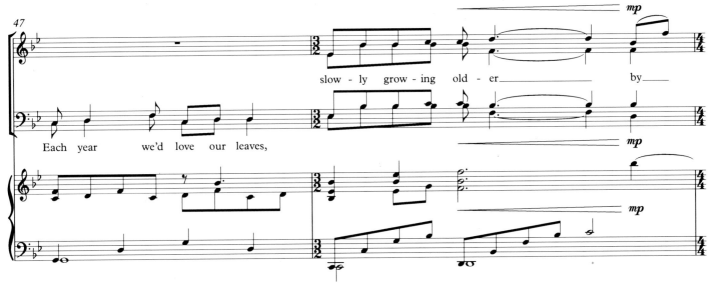

slow - ly grow - ing old - er_____ by_____

Each year we'd love our leaves,

poco rit.

let - ting them_____ go,   let - ting them_____ go._____

let - ting, by_____ let - ting them_____ go,_____   go._____

let - ting them   go,_____   go,_____   go._____

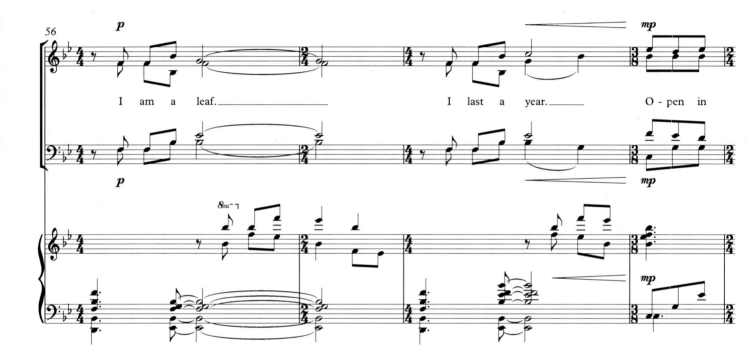

I am a leaf._____ I last a year._____ O - pen in

spring._____ Drop like a tear._____ My days are short.

They come and go._____ I feed on light,_____ so_____ a

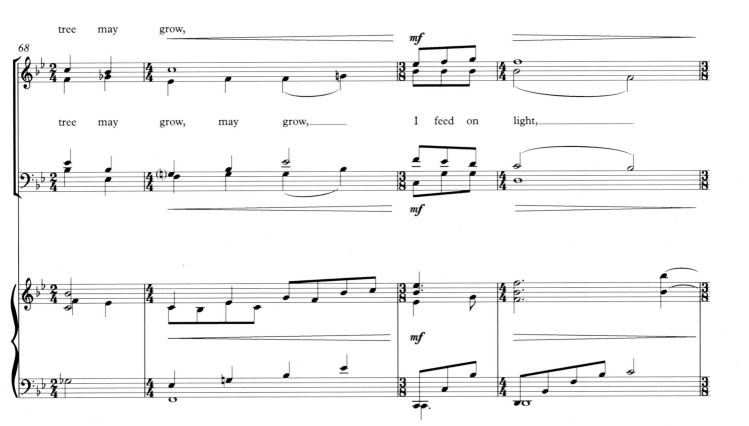

tree may grow,_____ mf

tree may grow, may grow,_____ I feed on light,_____

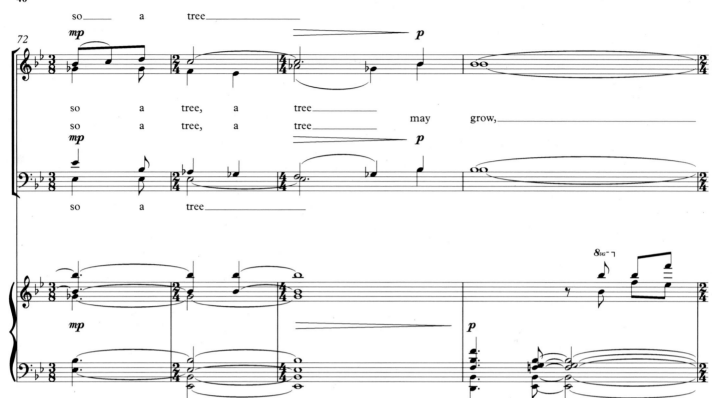

so____ a tree____

so a tree, a tree____ may grow,____
so a tree, a tree____

so a tree____

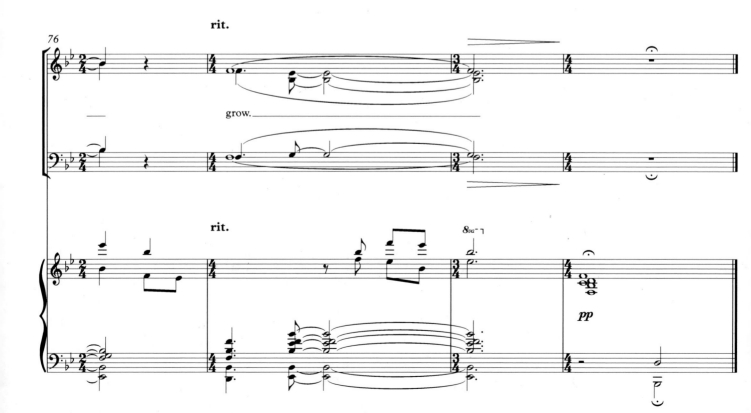

rit.

grow.____

rit.

pp